The Art of
Raymond Ching

Frontispiece CHARLEY-BARLEY; (Detail), actual size

The Art of Raymond Ching

Peter Hansard

COLLINS

Auckland Sydney Vancouver London

First published 1981
William Collins Publishers Ltd
Box 1, Auckland

© Raymond Ching 1981
ISBN 0 00 216974 x

Typeset by Queensland Type Service, Brisbane
Printed by Colorcraft, Hong Kong

Contents

List of Plates

9

The Art of
Raymond Ching

The Art of
Raymond Ching

SOME YEARS AGO, I accompanied Raymond Ching on a day trip to Rangitoto Island, a volcano in the Hauraki Gulf, New Zealand.

The trip was unusual in that I had finally managed to persuade the painter to leave his studio and enjoy a day in the sun and further, I even talked him aboard the small motor launch that plies the quiet waters of the gulf between Rangitoto and Auckland. (He has an aversion to boats that persists to this day.)

We had decided to take sketchbooks and experience the island for its own sake. Rangitoto is a volcanic lump, a symmetrical pile of raw scoria that forms a circle some ten kilometres across, and with a scanty covering of new bush struggling for a foothold on its stony slopes. Geologically speaking, the place is amazingly recent; Westminster Abbey, for instance, is some two hundred and fifty years older than Rangitoto.

During our long trek down the length of the island and back again (the abrasive surface of the scoria completely destroyed the soles of our shoes), Ching made many drawings of rocks, stunted plants, a very basic and sparse fantail nest, and the beach piled with boulders, driftwood and jetsam. I found the brightness of the sunlight almost unbelievable. The rocks were blackish, the bush black-green. Shadows were hard and impenetrable. Ching, it seemed to me, was able to draw objects quickly and accurately, remaining unconfused by the dense contrasts of the shadows, the bright reflective light and the infinite confusion of the myriad textures of twigs, leaves, water and stone.

The next day in his studio, while discussing the trip, he attempted to draw a prominent feature on the island in order to explain a point of view. I was astonished at the difficulty this caused him and at his apparent lack of interest in drawing anything at all from memory. That he was interested only in what he could *actually see*, was one of the first thoughts about the nature of his art ever to occur to me. There are many other peculiar traits in his approach. Not only does he not enjoy painting, he seldom ever thinks about it. For him, everything is drawing. (Fig. I seems to him, just as important as any other 'painting' in this book. As a matter of interest it is one of Ching's earliest 'bird' studies.)

'To say that I think about painting', he says with a shrug, 'might imply that I somehow intellectualise my work and that simply isn't true. I have only one painting in my head, and that's that.' So much for painting. But drawing?

'I really don't know how to explain my attitude to drawing. I'm genuinely sure I never look at anything without in some way immediately understanding how to draw it. I get this information fed into my brain even if I don't want it. It's entirely separate to painting. For instance, when I walk down the street with friends, I notice quite clearly that they don't react in the same way to what they see as I would. I can't even look at someone without seeing how to draw round the side of their face. It's most distracting and believe me, it has its drawbacks. I don't always follow what people are saying to me and I'm sure I appear vague and detached. I'm not saying this is some kind of unique ability but I am saying it's a fact. It haunts me all the time. It's really no wonder I draw every day, is it? I just can't switch off, it's all drawing.'

It's true that Ching's approach to art continually reflects such a pre-occupation, so much so that he even claims to feel happier about being confronted with a firm visual concept for a painting than if he were to sit down and think of one. He'd much rather draw what he actually sees than draw, so to speak, upon his imagination.

'In fact', he says, 'if you were to ask me if I wanted to draw, say, a tree, I'd honestly have to reply "No, not particularly." That would be true. I have no real interest in trees. But if I were then to walk down the path and see a gnarled branch hung with lichen and dappled with sunlight, I'd suddenly want to draw it. As an *idea*, no. But in *fact*, yes.'

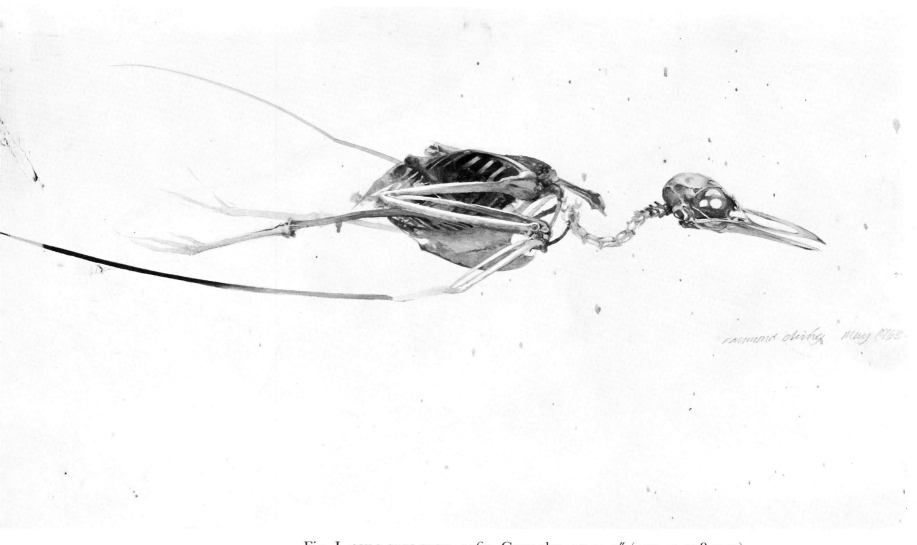

Fig. I. GULL SKELETON, 1963. Gouache, 17 × 9″ (432 × 228 mm)

Because his approach is so factual, and apart from painting his first interest is birdlife, any discussion on his art is going to be plagued by one particular area of argument. I refer to the usual prolegomenon which concerns itself with the old question of whether or not wildlife painting is 'art'. (Ching's skill in this area is such that it has not only brought him international acclaim, it has also been a major influence on the growing number of younger painters now working in this field.)

I believe the argument to be largely irrelevant, but ask Raymond Ching the same question and one receives direct and controversial answers. On the whole, he feels, most wildlife painting is 'regrettably boring'.

'I believe it does have a grand potential, but in my opinion, unfortunately, it is not often achieved. Bruno Liljefors, the Swedish painter working earlier this century, managed it, probably because he thought as a *painter*, rather than an *animal* painter.'

15

The Art of Raymond Ching

It's true that pictures of dead birds can be found in the museums of the world, while paintings of live birds are very much the exception. He feels there is good reason for this: 'Dead birds say something about man's intervention.' The point here of course, is that art always has something to do with the painter as an individual, not just what he paints. Such a painting tells you who the artist is, what he is, what he feels and what he thinks.

Dead birds arranged in decorative groups have their parallels in the floral arrangements that fit so easily into the still life art form. Living birds and animals somehow do not. They become an art subject rather than an art form. Traditional art forms such as the still life and the nude are, after all, very much contrivances that stem directly from the mind of the painter. Seldom, if ever, are they conceived as exact copies of the subject to be rendered faithfully as in real life—the painter invariably dramatises composition and colour, removes blemishes, adds grace and style, accentuates or diminishes form and generally in one way or another puts his or her own mark on the painting. That, indeed, is why it becomes a painting rather than an illustration.

Ching feels that perhaps the finest bird painting he has seen is the picture of a young hunter proudly holding up a dead bittern, the work of Rembrandt: 'It's quite exquisite, but why is that? Certainly because it's a Rembrandt and clearly because it is so human.'

One concludes from this that wildlife painting generally needs a hefty injection of individualistic style if it is to become 'art'. If so, one must recognise Ching's own work and his influence in this field as firmly leading the way.

That Ching puts so much emphasis on the painter rather than what he paints is no accident and it's an emphasis that applies equally to his own work which is so highly individualistic that it matters little if he paints a bird, a brick, a pool or a person. He claims to have been in pursuit of 'basically one painting, one concept', from the day he first began to paint.

'Look at my work', he says, 'and you'll see it conforms to the one set of rules, the one basic structure'. Of course his work is far more complex than that but nevertheless, one is able to refine it down to the idea of one form or subject usually isolated in some way against a detailed background

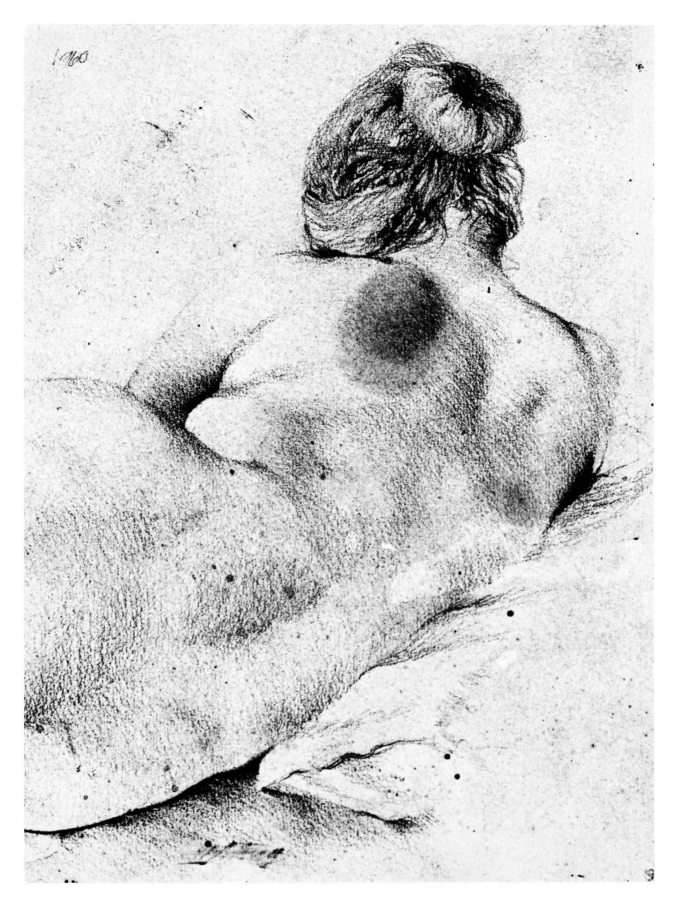

Fig. II. NUDE, 1960. Pencil, detail actual size

texture. Ideally, if the concept holds true, his paintings should look just as good and be just as pleasing hung upside down. In fact, I have seen him do just that with his pictures, turning them around to see if he likes them any better.

Like the writer whose final ambition is to write about absolutely nothing, Ching aims in the end to reduce everything he paints down to little more than the white ground of the panel or paper upon which he draws.

In fact Ching has come surprisingly close to this aim on a number of occasions. If one considers NEW WHITEWASH (Plate 18), for example, one sees that it deals with the complex technical problem of rendering weathered whitewash that is soiled and flaking on a wall lit with bright sunlight. At the corner of the building this wall butts up against a newly whitewashed wall which is mostly in shadow. Obviously there is an intriguing challenge involved in bringing this painting to a conclusion. Additionally, the dove roosting on the beam is white. But the picture is painted in transparent watercolour for the most part (a dash of gouache highlights the plaster on the wall at bottom right), so he has used only the smallest amount of white pigment. Most of the white you see is white paper. One wonders how he can use so little paint in the construction of what seems to be a highly detailed painting. Again it fits his basic rule—one object isolated against real and detailed texture. So the concept is really quite simple. The painting almost non-existent, yet it suggests something quite complex. This is the enigma that Ching offers us again and again . . . he himself is a complex person by nature, but one focussed absolutely on the problem of producing extremely simple paintings.

Ching would probably not wholly accept my contention that for him, paint gets in the way of things. He does, however, admit to a lifelong frustration with painting as opposed to drawing.

'I never desperately let myself down when I'm drawing', he says. 'The pencil is fine, it's an extension of me, so I can say pretty much what I mean when I'm drawing. But with my paintings I hardly ever do. Unfortunately they seem to end up full of those techniques, manners and contrivances which infuriate me. I like the painting well enough up to the final under-drawing but when the paint goes on, I find myself with the same old battle on my hands. As the work progresses it gets to be rather less than I had intended, less that I meant to say. Finally the painting becomes so distant

18

from my original intention that I call it finished because I can't really stand to see it anymore. Frankly, it shatters my confidence so much that I usually start another at once—rather like the wartime fighter pilots who are said to have been made to take to the air again immediately after a crash. For me, this approach works. As soon as I'm drawing again, my confidence returns because I can draw what I mean. That's where the frustration of it all lies for me—of course I can't just leave it as a drawing because one means to say more than that, and in paint. So I'm right back to square one. I'd have to say that with one or two exceptions, every painting I've ever done contains in my view, elements of failure. But I don't honestly think there is anything I can or should do about it.'

What he does do of course, is persist in his goal by seeking out those fleeting, rather momentary glimpses that generally make up the subject matter of his paintings, those candid visual fragments which in themselves are almost nothing, little pieces of time caught, held and thoroughly pared down to a kind of perfected simplicity. You see them over and over again in the pictures he has produced, particularly in the last seven or eight years.

Looking at these images, three points begin to emerge. First the vision itself. Whether he realises it or not, Ching avoids the ornate and in line with his own rather simple lifestyle, invariably opts for everyday, easily recognisable, one might say commonplace, subject matter. I know he'd much rather paint a sparrow than a peacock and although a painting of the latter is included in this volume (Plate 19), it is perhaps typical that he has painted the white form (his fascination with non-colours again) rather than the splendid plumage for which the bird is normally famous.

Secondly, there is the strange effect these simplified images often produce. They somehow invoke a sense of heightened reality because all extraneous considerations have been so cleverly stripped away. Nothing is included in these paintings that is not essential to the original concept.

And thirdly, there is the matter of the 'paint' which I have already discussed. Because the painter so sparingly uses pigment, his surfaces are uniformly smooth and flat, unblemished by impasto. Form and texture are always *drawn and painted in*, never simply suggested.

And so the enigma continues, for despite all I have said, Ching's paintings are not bare and colourless. Somehow they manage, in the end, to flow with a richness of spirit and a strong and forceful sense of completeness. They are positive paintings probably because we are all so highly conscious of the painter's personality when we look at them.

To use the example of the sparrow and the peacock once more, we see that he always dominates his subject matter to advantage. Looking at a painting of a peacock, the viewer would probably be conscious of two points: that the bird itself was a magnificent creature and that Ching had made a good job of painting it. In the case of the sparrow this does not happen. Sparrows seem such insignificant and nondescript birds, that the viewer concentrates solely upon the skill of the painting. The consideration is for Ching, not the subject. And I believe that he so often achieves this result because he draws upon such simple everyday images. People, wildlife, grass, skies, seas, the seasons . . . they are all around us and totally within our own experience, yet he manages to show them to us in such a direct fashion that we are forced to consider them anew.

The subject itself never takes control which is why, I suspect, he would much rather paint grass than orchids and why he seems to prefer to paint friends or relatives rather than fashionable or famous personalities. Far better in his mind, however unconscious of this approach he may be, that the painting exists first and where possible, the subject matter second.

For this reason, he is cursed with a love-hate attitude to drawing from the nude. Like many painters, drawings of the nude represent a large proportion of his work and have done for more than twenty years. However, such drawing demands a level of importance be placed upon the subject and he finds it difficult to explain his frustrations with it.

'If one is going to draw a blackbird, one has to get it right, even more right than, say, a bird of paradise. Everyone has seen a blackbird and hardly anyone has seen a bird of paradise, so errors in the blackbird drawing will be more noticeable and spoil any pleasure you may have in looking at it. But these considerations pale into insignificance when dealing with the human figure. Not only has everyone intimate knowledge of it, they have very definite feelings and emotions about it, and they run deep. A slight error in the blackbird drawing isn't really going to matter, is it? But errors in figure drawing, especially nudes, are not only noted, they can even be offensive. Bear in mind that I'm talking about *my* sort of drawing, whatever that is—I mean drawing not obviously distorted for any reason of style or technique, drawing that is supposed to be fairly accurately perceived.'

20

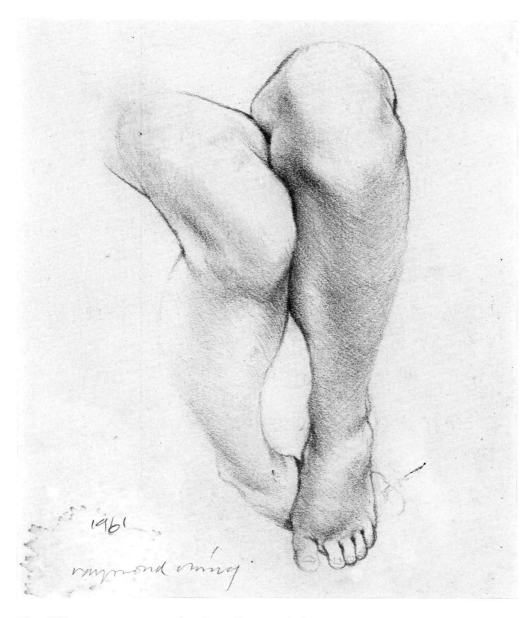

Fig. III. LEGS STUDY, 1961. Pencil, actual size

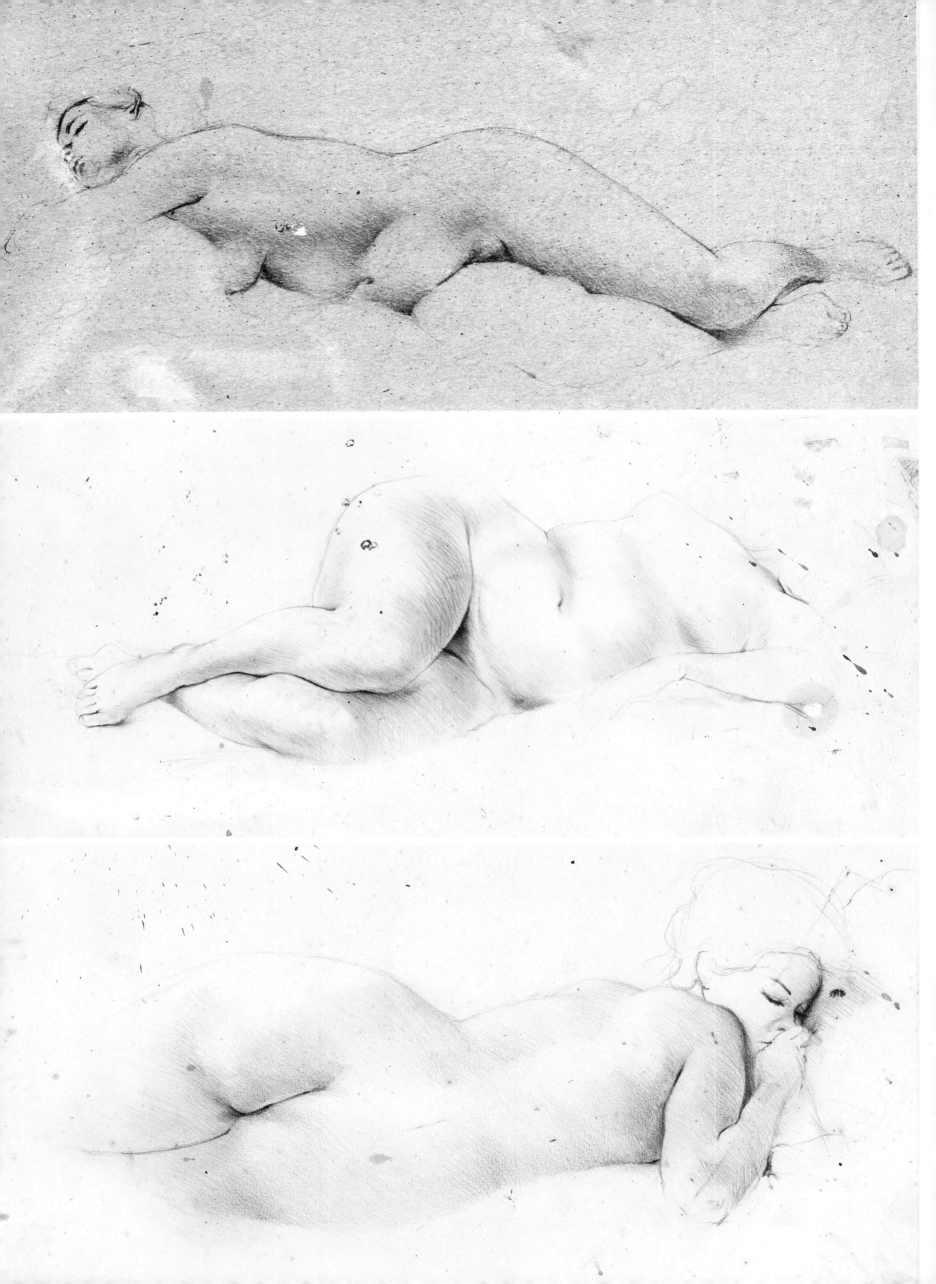

The Art of Raymond Ching

It's true that Ching's kind of drawing doesn't leave much margin for error and if, as he says, human reactions to the nude are deeply felt, one can see that his nudes are rather carefully drawn and are never ambiguous. They're worked out so that hopefully the viewer will agree that yes, within the terms of his or her own reference, Ching probably got it right.

Does this mean that he holds only to a fairly representational or accurate depiction of any given subject?

'Of course not', he says, 'there's always a natural distortion that one's own limitations, nervous system, optic nerves and brain cells bring about—that in the end is the real pleasure of it anyway—it's just that if the drawing of a nude seems unnatural or grotesque it becomes less acceptable than in most other subjects. Actually that's not really what I mean at all . . . look, when one draws or paints a picture, frames it and hangs it on the wall, one sets up a list of rules. Now what I'm saying is that the drawing will appear unnatural and grotesque if you don't stick to your own rules. I mean, you may well decide that both eyes should always be on the same side of the face, that lips are given a vertical bias and that breasts are square. That's all perfectly acceptable provided it hangs together, provided there's a kind of unity of thought and spirit running through the whole thing and the viewer sees it is so.

'Now the rules I set for myself and want the viewer to follow, are something I cannot change. You might term them "realistic" but that's a stupid word. Anyway, I'm stuck with *that* view of things. My nudes *have* to conform to those rules. They're difficult to produce because I insist on getting it right as quickly as I can, mainly because I'm so conscious of the model and my conviction that it can't possibly be much fun for her.

'Also, as I genuinely do little else but draw and paint and have no other interests, any sort of failure at drawing, the one thing I do most, is a major blow to my confidence.

'I try *not* to fail. But drawing from life is all about the risk of failure. So

Fig. IV. NUDE, 1960. Pencil, 11 × 20″ (280 × 508 mm)

Fig. V. NUDE, 1961. Pencil, 10 × 15½″ (254 × 394 mm)

Fig. VI. NUDE, 1961. Pencil, 11½ × 16″ (292 × 406 mm)

23

much so, that I've always thought I've had more chance of failing at nudes than any other thing I draw . . . when I draw them I really do get nervous and I don't feel good at all. I'm full of real trepidation every single time.'

Pressed to explain why this should be so, he answers this way: 'If I'm drawing a stone I have as much time as I want. It's going nowhere. When I draw a plant I have less time. It's fading, wilting and changing so I must draw faster and that is a little more difficult but it's also more exciting, for it clearly offers a greater potential for reward than the drawing of a stone. However, when I'm drawing a person who has voluntarily agreed to sit, nude, my involvement *really* becomes complex . . . for instance, one is hardly obligated to a plant but one is always obligated to the nude model. One is obliged to be considerate, to do one's best work. Not only that, the model is bound to get pins and needles in the left leg or something and have to move, so one is obliged to work very quickly. So with nudes, I find myself working *faster* than I want, on a subject far *harder* than normal and which carries more *responsibility*, if you like, than usual. For me to contend with these self-inflicted pressures requires strenuous consideration. On the other hand, on the rare occasions when I think I've made a good drawing, the pleasure in that achievement is unbeatable.'

This probably has something to do with the fact that Ching has seldom produced a painting of the nude. Although it is an art form he appreciates, it is not one in which he wishes to participate. There's a distinction here that Ching sees as important: 'I know I draw nudes but they're really an evasion because it's the naked I ought to be painting—and that's a totally different thing.' Here Ching is reflecting an attitude that stems from the old 'classical' versus 'romantic' arguments of the nineteenth century, an argument which has made even our realist painters of today so very different from painters of the past.

For outside the nude art form, the concept of a naked person becomes far more of a statement about what the artist and the model are thinking. The painter is revealed even more than the sitter for such work is of the inner mind, a reflection of the human condition, and while the nude can be sensual, the naked is invariably sexual.

Should Ching carry out such a painting, my guess is that it would have the simplicity of form and colour that appears in CHARLEY-BARLEY (Plate 4), somehow averting concern for the subject's nakedness and attempting, just

24

The Art of Raymond Ching

as CHARLEY-BARLEY does, to make one imagine what Ching thought that person was thinking at the time . . . all very complicated and such great fun and relevant here, for Ching's concern in this direction is reflected to some extent in this book. The nude drawing, Fig. II, now in possession of the Auckland City Art Gallery, is one of Ching's earliest life drawings. Plates 91, 92 and 93 are his most recent.

When it comes to Ching's personal preference in painting, his likes and dislikes, he feels that the older he gets the less he knows about anything. The old joke, 'I may know nothing about art, but I know what I like', seems fair enough to him. His own feelings about any given painting depend simply upon whether he feels 'It is right'.

He explains it this way, 'I stand in a gallery and I look at a painting and I think, "that's right!" It doesn't matter if it's a 14th century Giotto or an abstract expressionist or anything in between. Rarely, when I bring off a drawing I really like myself, I think, "that's right!" But I honestly don't know what I mean . . . except that it seems *undeniably* right, I mean you absolutely know it, for sure.'

Maybe once again, this is a further reflection of the importance he places on what he sees. A mathematician explaining a theory, or a philosopher outlining some esoteric argument could equally be greeted with the response, 'I see!' What the person means is, 'I understand'. In the same way, Ching is seeing, understanding and agreeing when he simply says, 'that's right'.

'I guess', says Ching, 'it would be extremely satisfying for me if I could produce a large simple painting of a single subject set in a complex yet uncomplicated space, using little colour and hardly any paint, and for people to look at it and say, "that's right!" If that sounds naive then I'm sorry, for me it's true and absolutely central to what I wish to achieve.'

Well, it's hard to be simple and even harder to get down to painting nothing. Does Ching really want to? Does he only ever paint one painting? It may interest readers to analyse this question for themselves and check out the design and composition of say CHRISTMAS DAY (Plate 7), and compare it with KINGFISHER (Plate 13), and WINTER GULL (Plate 45).

But the problem here is that I'm making it too simple. Because Ching himself admits to a constant fear of failure when painting, and because he has a real and driving need to paint every single day, failures can be destructive and undermine his confidence to a dramatic extent. This is

25

probably why he has found it hard to produce, say, more CHARLEY-BARLEYS and fewer birds. The plain facts of the matter are that birds represent a safe and disciplined order. He knows what he is about when he's painting them, he has a real passion for them, and he seldom fails at them.

Other paintings, portraits and landscapes, do exist for him but are approached with caution. He knows when he gets a firm image in his mind that it is only a matter of time before he will be driven to painting it. Unfortunately he also knows it will fail. 'I'm sure there's nothing unique in my predicament', Ching says. 'I guess it's something most painters live with. The truth is, it depresses me.'

So in order to paint every day with something approaching confidence, he returns to birds.

'It's no good saying to me, "Why do you keep on at birds—why don't you paint more people?" I paint what I paint and I can do only that. I don't think people realise just how much a painter is stuck with his own personality. He can never be other than what he is—of course he can't—anyway, one should never feel insecure about what one paints if one really wants to paint it. You see, I think that provided someone sincerely sets out to paint whatever he or she thinks is worth painting, then there's a measure of value in that painting. If it's the best that person can do, if it's his best shot, it shouldn't be arbitrarily dismissed. I'm not talking about money (that's a separate value system) but in human terms, such a painting has to be of value.'

Usually, painters get an idea about a subject and then sit down and through a series of drawings, studies and paintings, develop their ideas, their communications, into distinctive and recognisably personal statements about that subject. Normally the rendition of the subject itself is subordinate to the concept or the technique of painting and the overall message. Ching never does this for he seldom, if ever, has experimental themes in mind. He simply wants to draw an object and, in the act of drawing it, tell you that is what he wants to do— *to draw it*!

He even tells me that in the matter of portrait painting he seldom ever wants to chat to a sitter beforehand, as so many painters who wish to gauge something of a sitter's personality, are apt to do. 'I will tell you what I feel about a sitter's personality by the way I draw him—I don't have to speak to him, I just have to draw him. Apart from learning how to draw

26

the underlying anatomy, of having that understanding to some extent, I believe that things like character and personality are there on the surface and I don't wish to comment any further than that which my drawing shows me. I don't mean to sound arrogant—it's simply that there is no other way I can do it.'

So we have come full circle and once again, we are back to what is essentially *drawing*.

In conclusion, one has to say that Ching seems concerned with the ending of all things. The people he paints are conceived as time-battered personalities leaving, like the tide on the ebb, memory pools scattered behind them. In the paintings of Don Forrest for example, the pools are many and deep. In the paintings of his daughters, they are clear and fresh but still subject to the same dictates of time and nature.

The girl in the painting CHARLEY-BARLEY has lost what? Her youth, a lover, who knows? Ching offers us in these natural cycles, a real and substantial order, and in the best of his work, a celebration of values both worthwhile and familiar.

Selected Paintings
and Drawings

1. WAR PENSION, 1974

Watercolour, $24\frac{5}{8} \times 20\frac{1}{4}''$ (625 × 514 mm)

Collection: Mr R. G. Lawton

Wildlife painter Don Forrest came to England with the Canadian Army during the Second World War and never left. For many years he was a regular caller at Ching's studio on the edge of Romney Marsh, where, two or three times a week, his visits on an old motorbike would bring news of bird movements and any rarer species to be seen in the Sussex countryside.

In winter, the bleakness of the exposed marshes forced Don to wear upwards of three jackets and typically, they appear in each of his portraits.

2. PRE-STUDY FOR WAR PENSION, 1974
Pencil, $10\frac{1}{2} \times 13''$ (267 × 330 mm)
Collection: Errol Fuller Esq.

3. BACK STUDY, 1975
Pencil, 10½ × 8½″ (267 × 216 mm)
Collection: Mr B. Lewis

A pre-study for the water-colour,
CHARLEY-BARLEY.

4. CHARLEY-BARLEY, 1975

Watercolour, 26½ × 21½″ (673 × 546 mm)

Collection: Mrs R. Porter

During the several days taken to complete this
picture, the artist's son, learning his first nursery
songs, sang the rhyme of Charley-Barley over
and over again. The artist and the model found
themselves so obsessed with the tune that in the
end, it was agreed the painting should receive
this unusual title.

This watercolour is perhaps the most
universally admired of all Ching's work from the
seventies and has been reproduced in print the
world over.

5. LOUISE, 1977

Pencil, 13 × 11½″ (330 × 292 mm)

Private collection

6. WAVE STUDIES, 1976

Pencil, 20 × $12\frac{3}{4}''$ (508 × 324 mm)

Private collection

7. CHRISTMAS DAY (Morning Tide), 1976

Watercolour, 29 × 21″ (736 × 533 mm)

Collection: Mr and Mrs G. Chote

When painting this watercolour on the busy
English coast one high summer in July, the
artist found himself flooded with memories of
Christmas. This of course, is a reflection of his
expatriate condition, for Christmas in New
Zealand is strongly associated with summer and
the beach—though in his homeland, the isolated
coves and inlets that Ching favoured are a far
cry from the bustling crowds of Dover.

8. HEAD, PRE-STUDY FOR CHRISTMAS DAY, 1976
Watercolour, 12 × 12″ (305 × 305 mm)
Private collection

9. DRESS STUDY FOR CHRISTMAS DAY, 1976
Pencil, 18 × 13″ (457 × 330 mm)
Private collection

10. PRE-STUDY FOR THE EXPATRIATE, 1974

Oil, on prepared panel, 14 × 11″
(335 × 279 mm)

Collection: Mr A. L. Marquet

11. THE EXPATRIATE, 1974
Oil, $22\frac{1}{4} \times 22\frac{3}{4}''$ (564 × 578 mm)
Collection: Mr J. W. Cropper

12. COBWEBS 2, 1973

Watercolour, $10\frac{1}{2} \times 8\frac{1}{2}''$ (267 × 216 mm)

Collection: Dr R. M. Bernau

Pre-study for the top right hand corner of a barn window used in the 1973 watercolour WINTER WRENS.

Drawn directly from nature, sketches of this kind are later repainted in the studio as carefully planned elements in final paintings.

13. KINGFISHER, 1978

Oil, on panel, 19 × 14″ (482 × 355 mm)

Collection: Patrician Art

This is the European Kingfisher, *Alcedo atthis*,
less readily seen than its New Zealand
counterpart *Halcyon sancta* and less often painted
by Ching. One of a pair of small paintings, the
study was made from a bird which killed itself
flying into a window. The water splash was
developed from a series of drawings made from
running the studio tap into a spoon.

14. WILD DUCK, 1975

Oil, on prepared panel, $14\frac{1}{2} \times 11''$
(368 × 279 mm)

Collection: Mr I. Anson

Painted on a small farm pond at Peashmarsh
near Rye, this is the first of a continuing series,
both in watercolour and oil, showing birds
moving in water. The bird usually chosen is
either a pochard or mallard duck, but the species
is less important than the effect of its movements
on the water.

15. MALLARD, 1977

Oil, on prepared panel, 13 × 10″
(330 × 254 mm)

Collection: D. E. G. Munro Esq.

16. ECLIPSE POCHARD, 1977

Oil, on panel, $13\frac{1}{2} \times 10''$ (343 × 254 mm)

Collection: D. E. G. Munro Esq.

17. DOMESTIC FOWLS, 1974

Pencil, $17\frac{1}{2} \times 13\frac{3}{4}''$ (444 × 350 mm)

Private collection

These fowls and the peacock and doves (Plates 18, 19, 20), are domestic birds kept by a friend of the artist in a courtyard of fifteenth century farmbuildings in North Wales. They represent some of the very few studies made by the artist of domesticated birds.

18. NEW WHITEWASH, 1974

Watercolour and acrylic on paper, 27 × 20″
(685 × 508 mm)

Private collection

19. WHITE PEACOCK, 1974

Acrylic, on paper, 26 × 27″ (660 × 685 mm)

Private collection

20. MAIN HOUSE, 1976

Watercolour and gouache, 27 × 21″
(685 × 533 mm)

Private collection

21. TIDE, 1976

Watercolour and gouache, $19\frac{1}{2} \times 28''$
(495 × 711 mm)

Collection: Bill Double Esq.

22. PLOVER CHICKS, 1976

Watercolour, $20\frac{3}{4} \times 28''$ (528 × 711 mm)

Collection: Bill Double Esq.

Both this work and the preceding TIDE study
were carried out in the three days, 8, 9 and 10
May, 1976, at Winchelsea beach, near the
painter's Sussex studio. The illusion of a shallow
tide receding over the sand is unexpectedly
carried out in dry-brush, without overpainting,
both the water and the sand it covers being
rendered in small strokes at one and the same
time.

23. FIELD TRACK, 1975

Acrylic with oil on prepared panel, 13 × 10″
(330 × 254 mm)

Collection: Mrs K. Strevens

24. CLAY BANK, 1975

Gouache, 20 × 29¼″ (508 × 742 mm)

Collection: Mr J. E. Sparrow

A pre-study for SPARROWHAWK DUSTING, oil,
1975.

25. WOOD FRINGES, 1974

Oil, on panel, 14 × 12″ (355 × 304 mm)

Collection: Mr T. S. Newland

The making of this small picture was more than
usually complicated and spread over a period of
many months. The flash pools which had
prompted the painting began to dry up as work
progressed and never returned, for this was the
year of the worst droughts recorded in southern
Britain. There is, therefore, evidence of re-
working and overpainting, unusual for Ching.

26. DARK STEPS, 1973
Acrylic, 18 × 14″ (457 × 355 mm)
Collection: Mrs J. G. Tedcastle

27. DOVE IN A LOFT, 1976

Watercolour, 25 × 21″ (635 × 533 mm)

Collection: Mr Ian Bond

The last, and certainly most abstract, of the series of dove paintings made in Wales, this picture is probably most characteristic too, for the rendering of old whitewashed stone in pure watercolour demands that the work be undertaken without the use of white paint or any overpainting. Only the shadows and chips of texture are actually painted on the surface (see also the sheets in CHARLEY-BARLEY (Plate 4)); much of the painting's freshness of impact, stems from the resulting illusion.

28. BLOOMSBURY GROUP, 1975

Watercolour, 23 × 28″ (584 × 711 mm)

Collection: Mr R. W. Haworth

Barbara Bagenal has for ten years been a neighbour of the artist in the ancient town of Rye. Now possibly the last surviving member of the famed 'Bloomsbury Group' of English writers, painters and philosophers who made such an impact in the early part of this century, Barbara is mentioned in the diaries and biographies of Virginia Woolf and was a close friend of her sister, Vanessa Bell.

She endeared herself to the Woolfs by working tirelessly and cheerfully at the Hogarth Press, and it was during this period that Barbara set the type for the first edition of Katherine Mansfield's *Prelude*, a copy of which she still values. She lived at this time in the same block of flats as Katherine and Middleton Murry and speaks of Katherine with affection.

This portrait was developed from number of smallish drawings and studies, each of necessity taking no longer than ten or fifteen minutes because Barbara, now in her eighties, suffers from arthritis. The sittings were made particularly pleasurable for the artist by her many personal anecdotes of such famous figures as E. M. Forster, Lytton Strachey, Dora Carrington, Roger Fry, Bertrand Russell, Duncan Grant, David Garnett, Desmond MacCarthy and other prominent personalities associated with the Bloomsbury Group.

82

29. PRE-STUDY FOR BLOOMSBURY GROUP, 1975

Acrylic, $10\frac{1}{2} \times 5\frac{1}{2}''$ (267 × 140 mm)

Private collection

30. COLETTE, 1977

Watercolour, 19 × 14¾″ (482 × 375 mm)

Collection: The artist

The artist's elder daughter, Colette, was born in 1961 and this portrait of her (reproduced actual size) was painted in Wellington, New Zealand, when she was aged sixteen years.

At this time, the artist also completed the study of his younger daughter, Rachel (Plate 31).

31. RACHEL, 1977

Watercolour, $18\frac{1}{2} \times 14\frac{1}{2}''$ (470 × 368 mm)

Collection: The artist

The artist's younger daughter, aged fourteen
years.

32. HARE, 1978

Oil on prepared panel, $14\frac{1}{4} \times 13\frac{1}{2}''$
(362 × 343 mm)

Private collection

33. CUT FLOWERS, 1975

Watercolour, 19 × 25″ (482 × 635 mm)

Private collection

The theme is a recurring one—life, decay, renewal.

34. SHEEP SKULL, 1972

Transparent watercolour and pencil,
$9\frac{1}{4} \times 13\frac{3}{4}''$ (234 × 350 mm)

Collection: Eroll Fuller Esq.

35. FLEDGLING ROOK, 1972

Watercolour, 15 × 11½" (381 × 292 mm)

Collection: C. Sinclair-Smith

Never intended for development into finished paintings, watercolour 'drawings' of this kind are made essentially for the painter's own instruction and seldom find their way out of the studio.

The bird is a fledgling of the European Rook *Corvus frugilegus* and the study is, as usual, drawn direct from nature and life-size.

36. HANDS. PRE-STUDIES FOR KIRI, 1974

Pencil, $12\frac{1}{2} \times 19\frac{1}{2}''$ (317×495 mm)

Private collection

37. KIRI, 1974

Watercolour, 24 × 21½″ (609 × 546 mm)

Collection: Mr R. G. Lawton

The artist and now internationally acclaimed
opera singer, Miss Kiri Te Kanawa, first met in
London in the late sixties. Embarking on what
was to become common working practice, Ching
carried out a large number of drawings during
several sittings and developed the painting itself
later, in his studio.

38. PRE-STUDY FOR KIRI, 1974
Pencil, 11 × 15″ (279 × 381 mm)
Collection: Mr and Mrs B. Collinson

39. PETER HANSARD, 1977
Pencil, $17\frac{3}{4} \times 14\frac{3}{4}''$ (451 × 375 mm)
Private collection

40. PRE-STUDY FOR PORTOBELLO ROAD, 1977

Pencil, $17 \times 12\frac{1}{2}''$ (431×317 mm)

Private collection

Ching's home and studio was, for a number of
years, above an antique shop in London's
Portobello Road. Later for several years his
second wife, Louise, owned a stall there dealing
in antique jewellery. The artist's drawings of the
road capture the cold winter days—people
wrapped in furs, or sitting with feet tucked
inside cardboard boxes to keep out the chill and
draughts.

41. WOMAN WITH SHELLS, 1977

Pencil, $17 \times 13\frac{1}{2}''$ (431 × 343 mm)

Private collection

42. WAVE STUDY, 1976

Watercolour, $7\frac{1}{2} \times 11''$ (190 × 280 mm)

Collection: Mrs M. P. Webster

43. WAVE, 1976

Watercolour, $7\frac{1}{2} \times 11''$ (190 × 280 mm)

Collection: Mrs A. F. Laity

44. WAVE, 1976

Watercolour, $8 \times 11''$ (203 × 280 mm)

Collection: Mr A. L. Marquet

The New Zealand poet Basil Dowling's poem *Nowhere far from the sea* probably explains the recurrence of this subject in Ching's work as well as anything. Like most New Zealanders, Ching has always lived close to the sea and a large proportion of his work reflects this environment.

45. WINTER GULL, 1977

Oil, on prepared gesso panel, 19 × 14″
(482 × 355 mm)

Collection: D. E. G. Munro Esq.

The dark brown beak and black iris show this
New Zealand gull to be still in juvenile plumage,
with the distinctive red bill and silver-white
eye as yet undeveloped. The decision to ignore
the common and more brightly coloured adults
of this species, in favour of an immature bird
with its duller plumage, is almost certainly a
conscious one. The use of violent colour is usually
rejected by Ching and this near monochromatic
picture is perfectly characteristic.

46. SEA STUDY, 1977
Watercolour, 13 × 8½″ (330 × 216 mm)
Private collection

47. GULL STUDIES, 1977
Pencil, 10 × 13½″ (254 × 343 mm)
Private collection

48. GULLS, 1977
Pencil, 7½ × 17½″ (190 × 444 mm)
Private collection

49. GULL STUDIES, 1977
Pencil, 11¾ × 17¼″ (298 × 438 mm)
Private collection

Without exception, the species of gull shown in
Ching's paintings is *Larus novaehollandiae*, the New
Zealand red-billed gull. Drawing after drawing
show these birds in summer and winter dress,
immature and adult, from time to time
developed into a full painting but more often
left as drawings; probably not made through
any special affection for these birds, but simply
because they are always there—and more
importantly for the artist, they are not shy and
may be drawn from life at close quarters.

50. PACIFIC GULL, 1977

Watercolour, dry-brush, $28\frac{1}{2} \times 20\frac{1}{2}''$
(724×520 mm)

Collection: R. G. Lawton

The title of this painting evokes the concept of
Ching's fondly remembered New Zealand
beaches and estuaries facing the Pacific Ocean.
The bird is not of course the large Pacific gull
found in Australia, but once again the small,
ubiqitous red-billed gull—for Ching, very much
the 'gull of the Pacific'.

51. GULLS, 1979

Pencil, $19\frac{1}{2} \times 13''$ (495 × 330 mm)

Private collection

52. STUDIES OF CLOUDS, 1976
Watercolour, 19 × 23″ (483 × 584 mm)
Courtesy, International Art Centre

53. STUDY OF CLOUDS, 1976
Watercolour, 20 × 30″ (508 × 762 mm)
Collection Mrs J. D. Moleta

54. CLOUDS, 1977
Watercolour, 20 × 30″ (508 × 762 mm)
Collection: Mrs C. Harvey

55. STARTLED PARTRIDGE, 1976

Oil, on prepared panel, 19 × 16″
(483 × 407 mm)

Collection: Mr A. L. Marquet

A study of the grey partridge *Perdix perdix*,
flushed and rising directly from hedgerow cover.
The characteristic whirring of its short wings is
easily imagined.

56. DON FORREST, 1976

Oil on panel, $13\frac{1}{2} \times 10\frac{3}{4}''$ (342 × 267 mm)

Collection: M. H. Allen

The last in the series of paintings and drawings
of the artist's friend Don Forrest, made a year
or so before his death.

Not greatly larger than reproduced here, this
small picture was painted at the Rye studio over
a period of three or four afternoons.

The low winter light moving quickly around
the room is almost certainly the reason for parts
of this painting showing evidence of more
changes and re-working than is usual, and by
troubling for only slight resolution of the sitter's
jacket and clothing, Ching has allowed himself
to concentrate almost solely on the closely
observed head.

57. BLACKBIRD, 1976

Oil on panel, 14 × 11″ (355 × 279 mm)

Collection: Mr and Mrs W. J. Harvey

With this small work, Ching is again painting
the unchanging cycles of nature but with
perhaps more poignancy than usual, for here the
bird's death is felt almost as a personal blow.
Painted at the end of summer, this complex but
uncomplicated picture creates a world of hard
ground, sticks and fallen leaves, of which the
cock bird now becomes inevitably a part.

58. PRE-STUDY FOR BLACKBIRD, 1976
Pencil, 15 × 12″ (381 × 304 mm)
Private collection

59. PRE-STUDY FOR BLOOD AND FIRE, 1977

Pencil, 12 × 16¼″ (304 × 412 mm)

Private collection

Mrs Rhoda Ching, the artist's mother, had
served in the Salvation Army for over fifty
years when the artist painted her in her
seventy-fourth year. The bonnet's unfaded
colour reflects its newness, prompted by the
occasion of sitting for her portrait.

60. BLOOD AND FIRE, PORTRAIT OF THE ARTIST'S
MOTHER, 1977

Watercolour, $24\frac{1}{2} \times 20\frac{1}{2}''$ (622 × 520 mm)

Private collection

61. HANDS. PRE-STUDY FOR BLOOD AND FIRE, 1977

Pencil, 11 × 7″ (279 × 178 mm)

Private collection

62. QUILL, 1977
Pencil, $14\frac{3}{4} \times 11\frac{1}{2}''$ (375 × 292 mm)
Collection: The artist

The artist's son, aged five years.

63. ANN HAMILTON, 1979

Pencil, 17 × 12″ (432 × 304 mm)

Private collection

Miss Hamilton is a neighbour of Ching's in the
cobbled lanes and sixteenth century houses of the
medieval town of Rye in Sussex.

64. MISS HAMILTON, CHURCH SQUARE, 1979
Watercolour, 27 × 21″ (685 × 533 mm)
Private collection

65. BOTANY BAY, 1976

Gouache, 26 × 21″ (660 × 533 mm)

Collection: Dr J. B. McGeachen

For generations, Doug Child's family have lived
and worked in the country towns of Sussex, but
the lack of opportunity in the area finally forced
him to seek a new life abroad. He sat for this
painting shortly before leaving for Australia
with his wife and young family.

66. SHEETS AND PILLOWS, PRE-STUDY FOR
SUMMER FIRES, 1977

Pencil, $11\frac{1}{2}$ × 10″ (292 × 254 mm)

Private collection

67. PILLOWS, 1977

Pencil, 12 × 20″ (304 × 508 mm)

Private collection

68. PRE-STUDY FOR SUMMER FIRES, 1977
Watercolour, 20 × 28″ (508 × 711 mm)
Collection: Mr A. C. Fay

69. WHITE NIGHTGOWN, PRE-STUDY FOR
SUMMER FIRES, 1978

Watercolour and gouache, 20 × 16″
(508 × 406 mm)

Collection: Louise Ching

70 SUMMER FIRES, 1978
Watercolour, 28 × 22″ (711 × 558 mm)
Private collection

71. PRE-STUDY FOR SUMMER FIRES, 1978

Pencil, $19\frac{1}{2} \times 13\frac{1}{2}''$ (495×343 mm)

Private collection

72. WINTER WREN, 1978

Oil, on panel, 14 × 11″ (355 × 279 mm)

Collection: Mary B. Fink

A common wren seeks warmth from the thin,
winter sun. Ching has always thought it more
than worthwhile to follow such familiar species
throughout the year, to draw them over and
again for their subtle changes of behaviour and
appearance through the seasons—the fine
plumage of summer; the frayed tail feathers
after nesting; their shyness in hedgerows during
the moult; their isolation in winter.

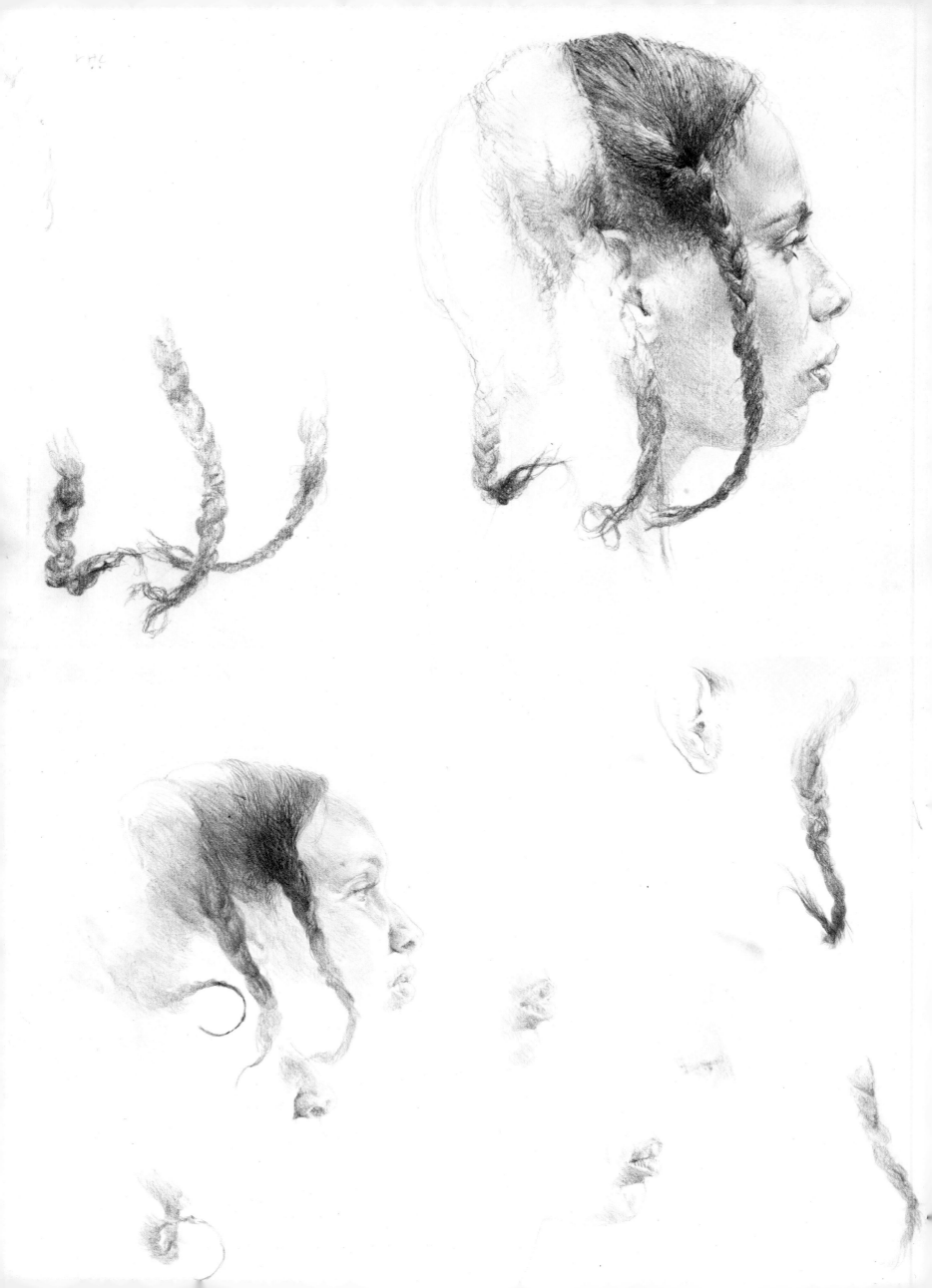

73. VANESSA. PRE-STUDY, 1978
Pencil, 12½ × 17″ (317 × 432 mm)
Private collection

74. VANESSA. PRE-STUDY, 1978
Pencil, 12½ × 16″ (317 × 406 mm)
Private collection

75. VANESSA, 1978

Watercolour, $25\frac{3}{4} \times 21\frac{1}{4}''$ (654×539 mm)

Private collection

76. VANESSA. PRE-STUDY, 1978
Pencil, $12\frac{1}{2} \times 9\frac{1}{4}''$ (317 × 235 mm)
Collection: Vanessa Thompson

77. CHRISTINE TATTERSFIELD. PRE-STUDY, 1979
Pencil, 17 × 12″ (432 × 304 mm)
Private collection

78. CHRISTINE TATTERSFIELD, 1979

Watercolour, 28 × 21½″ (711 × 546 mm)

Private collection

There is a gap of more than fifteen years between
this fine large watercolour and Ching's other
commissioned portraits, which were all
undertaken in the painter's early twenties. Such
earlier works were usually rendered in tempera
or oil, on a much smaller scale.

79. CHRISTINE TATTERSFIELD. PRE-STUDY, 1979

Pencil, $18\frac{3}{4} \times 13\frac{3}{4}''$ (476 × 349 mm)

Private collection

80. PRE-STUDIES FOR COUNTRY GIRL, 1972
Pencil, 18 × 12″ (457 × 304 mm)
Collection: Delia Benmax

81. COUNTRY GIRL, 1972
Acrylic on paper, 20 × 27½″ (508 × 698 mm)
Courtesy, International Art Centre

82. CAROLYN, 1979
Pencil, 19 × 13¼″ (482 × 336 mm)
Private collection

A presentation drawing, not made in preparation
for a painted work, but complete in itself.

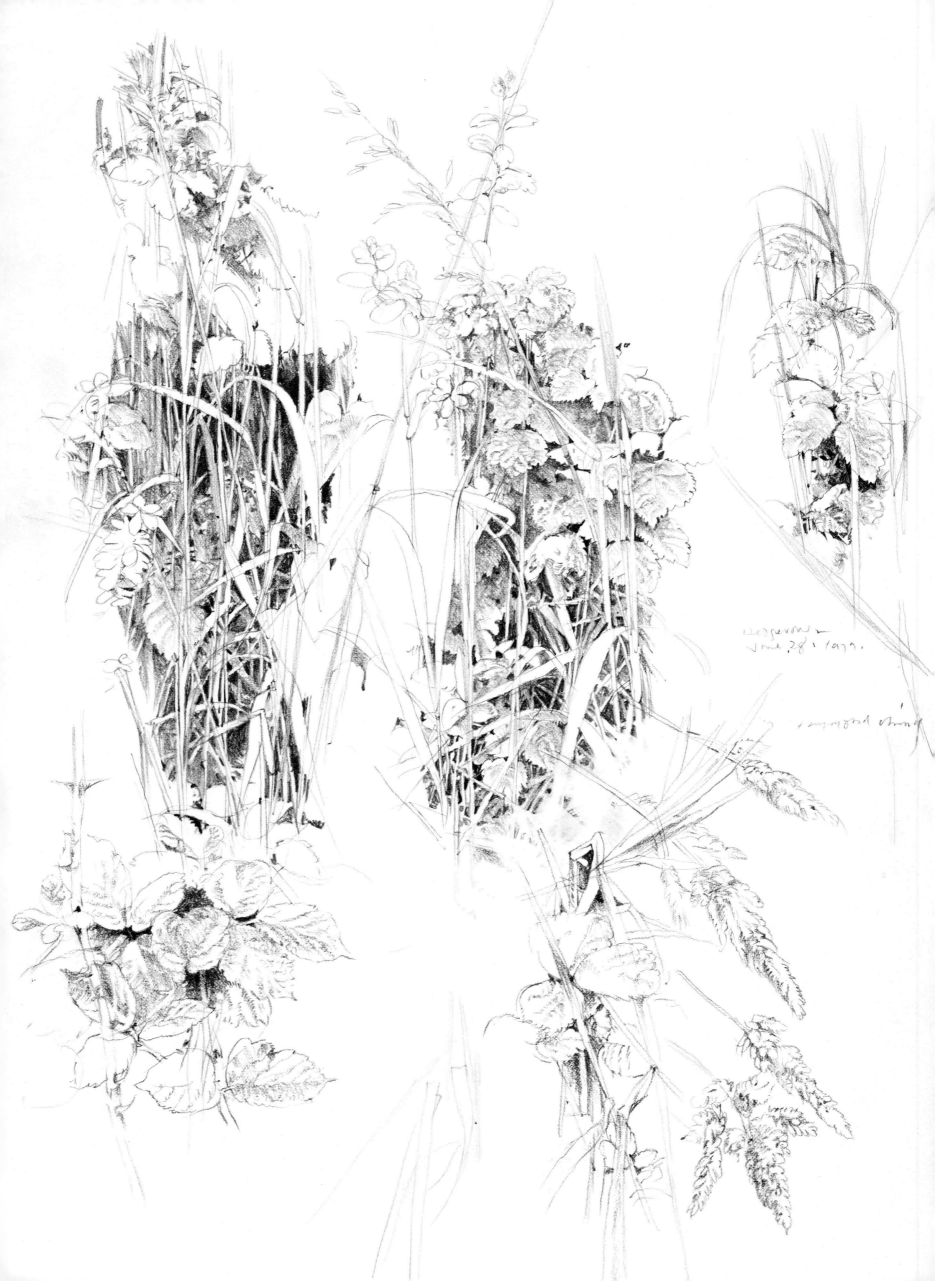

83. GRASS STUDIES FOR PARTRIDGE IN HEDGEROW, 1979

Pencil, 21 × 14½″ (533 × 368 mm)

Private collection

84. PARTRIDGE IN HEDGEROW, 1979

Acrylic, on paper, $28\frac{3}{4} \times 21\frac{5}{8}''$ (730 × 549 mm)

Collection: Russell A. Fink Esq.

The status of the partridge has changed from a
quite common bird, to one whose survival is
increasingly threatened. This study, painted in
high summer with acrylic as the medium,
allowed the artist to waive the usual restrictions
of a highly planned watercolour and employ the
more spontaneous possibilities of overpainting.

85. PARTRIDGES. PRE-STUDY, 1979

Pencil, 18 × 12″ (457 × 304 mm)

Private collection

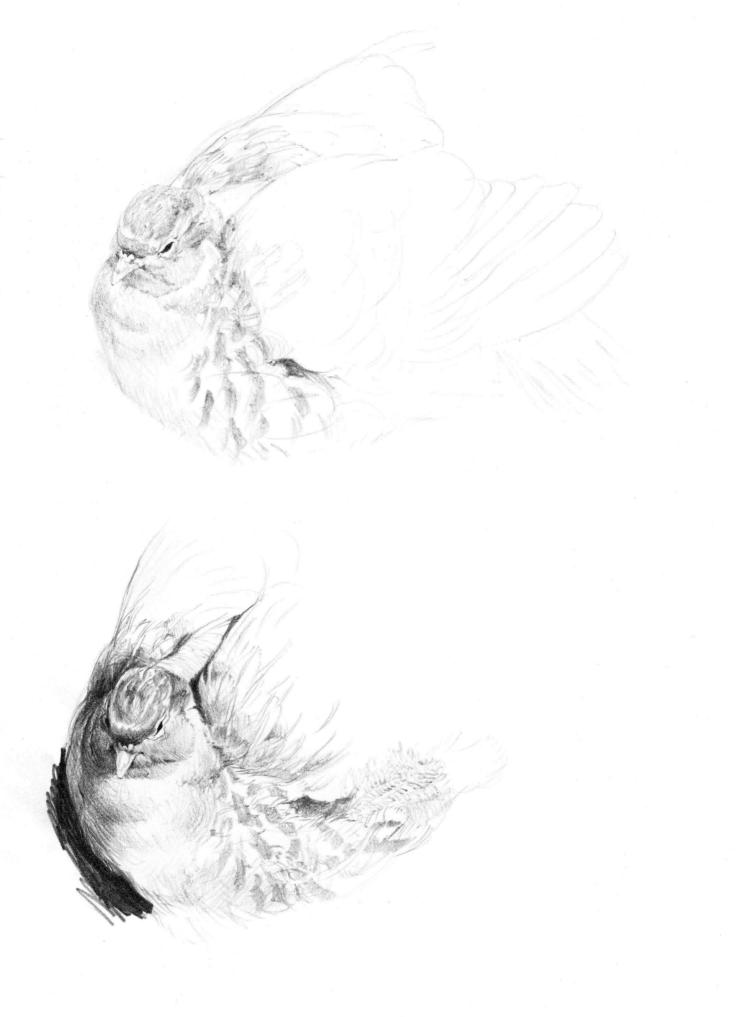

86. OAK LEAVES, 1979

Pencil, 20 × 14″ (508 × 355 mm)

Private collection

oak

August 28, 1954.

87. THISTLE, 1979

Pencil, $18\frac{1}{4}$ × $12\frac{1}{4}''$ (463 × 311 mm)

Private collection

A background study made specifically for a painting of European goldfinches, this pencil drawing is accompanied by colour notes and details of size. An individual species such as this may be drawn many times throughout the year, to note seasonal changes.

So much of Ching's output is related to his obsessive curiosity with the natural order and hundreds of species drawings of trees, flowering plants, grasses etc., lying in untidy heaps around his studio, are a reflection of this interest.

88. NUDE STUDY, 1975

Pencil, 20 × 15″ (508 × 381 mm)

Collection: Mrs Carol Childs

89. NUDE, 1979
Pencil, 24 × 15″ (609 × 381 mm)
Private collection

90. NUDE, 1979
Pencil, 27 × 17″ (685 × 431 mm)
Private collection

91. NUDE, 1979
Pencil, 19 × 14″ (482 × 355 mm)
Private collection

92. NUDE, 1979
Pencil, 27 × 18″ (685 × 457 mm)
Collection: Mr K. L. Maynard-Clarke

93. NUDE, 1979
Pencil, 27 × 17½″ (685 × 444 mm)
Collection: Mr K. L. Maynard-Clarke

Acknowledgments

THE AUTHOR is indebted to the many galleries and collectors who so willingly supplied details of size and medium of works in their possession, and who assisted in many ways for their paintings to be made available for reproduction in this book.

My thanks to Marti Friedlander for permission to reproduce her photograph of Raymond Ching.

Copyright Notice